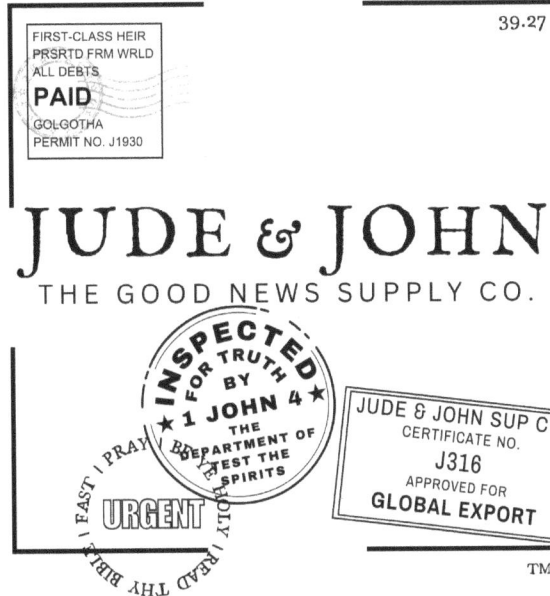

Milk, Cookies, and The Messiah
Copyright © 2025 by Jude and John Publishing
Authored by Lakeisha Little.
All rights reserved.

ISBN: 979-8-9931916-0-7

For more information visit
www.JudeAndJohn.com

Printed in U.S.A.

The lunch bell rang and the hallways of Gingersnap Community School filled with hungry students.

Eden found her spot at the lunch table and opened her lunchbox. Inside were all of her favorites: a sandwich, a shiny red apple, and a bunch of chocolate chip cookies.

Right on top was a little note with a Bible verse written on it. The note was from Eden's mom. Reading it was Eden's favorite part of the school day.

"What's that paper?" asked Melody.

"It's a Bible verse," said Eden. "My mom puts one in my lunch every day."

"Ooh, that's cool." Melody said. "What's it say today?"

Eden read aloud: "Jesus is the bread of life."

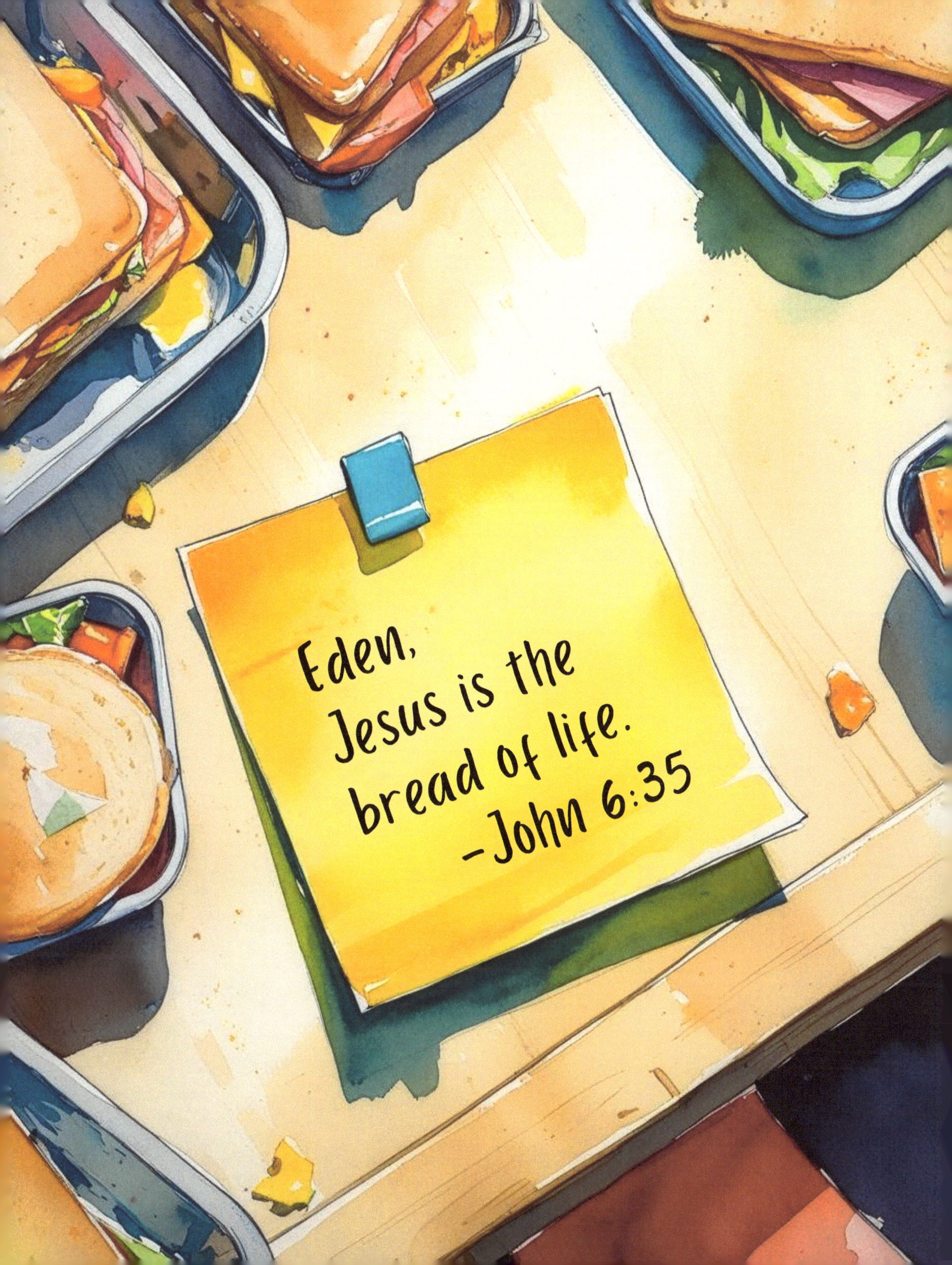
Eden,
Jesus is the
bread of life.
-John 6:35

"What does 'Bread of Life' mean?" Melody asked. "Like... a sandwich? Was Jesus a loaf of bread or something?"

"No!" Eden laughed. "Not like toast or sandwiches. Jesus didn't mean that kind of bread."

They both giggled.

Eden explained, "Back when Jesus was on Earth, bread was something people ate every day. It filled them up and gave them energy. So when Jesus said, 'I am the Bread of Life,' He meant that He fills our hearts and helps us live for God and be close to Him."

Zainab, Eden's classmate, tilted her head and asked, "But why do you need Jesus to do that?"

Eden scooted closer. "The Bible says God is holy, and we've all done wrong things called sin. Sin separates us from God. But Jesus came to fix that."

Zainab said, "In Islam, we believe God is one and powerful, but you can't get close to Him. He's too holy."

Eden nodded. "God is holy. But the Bible says He wants to be close to us, so Jesus came to bring us near. He's like a bridge that helps us get back to God and stay connected with Him."

Zainab's eyes widened. "Really? So you believe you can be close to God?"

"Yes!" Eden said with a smile. "When we trust Jesus, we become part of God's family, and we're close to Him for like, ever."

Zainab's friend, Yasmin, had been listening from across the table. She didn't wear a head covering, but she was muslim like Zainab.

Yasmin leaned into the conversation and said, "In my family we recite prayers five times a day on a special mat, and we have to face a certain direction. That's how we connect to God."

"That sounds special," Eden said kindly. "I talk to God too, but through Jesus. With Jesus, you can pray anytime, anywhere. Even wearing pajamas while riding a rollercoaster with a lion!"

Everyone at the table giggled.

Eden continued. "Jesus made it so that we can always be near God. No mat, no special place, just Him," she said.

Yusuf, who was also muslim, looked thoughtful and said, "My dad always says that Jesus was a prophet. That's what we learn in our family."

Eden smiled gently. "I get that Yusuf, but the bible says that Jesus is more than a prophet. He's God's Son. He came from Heaven, lived a perfect life without ever doing anything wrong, and then He died on the cross to take the punishment for all the wrong things we've ever done."

Eden paused and her eyes sparkled. She raised her voice with excitement. "And the best part? After three days, He came back to life! It's like the greatest surprise ever!"

Yusuf's eyes grew wide. "Wow, sounds like Jesus might have saved the world!"

Everyone giggled.

Sitting near Yusuf were Jewish sisters: Rachel, Leah, and Esther. They had been listening to the conversation.

"We're still waiting for the Messiah to come," said Rachel.

"Oh, but Jesus is the Messiah! He already came said," Eden replied.

Rachel frowned. "But if He already came, why don't we do things differently now? In our family, we have really hard rules to follow to stay close to God. The rules are supposed to make us right with Him until the Messiah comes."

Eden listened carefully. "Yeah, some people don't believe Jesus is the Messiah, so they still follow God the old way with rules and stuff. But Jesus really is the Messiah, and He already came to make a way for us to be accepted by God, not by just following rules, but by believing in Him."

Rachel thought quietly.

"Wait," Leah said gently. "So... you don't have to earn God's love? Like... ever?"

Eden grinned, "Nope! God loves us no matter what. And we can't earn His love by following rules perfectly. Jesus already took care of that when He died for us. When we believe in Him, we're made right with God not by rules, but by His love and grace."

"Wow! So... no more rules?!" Esther questioned with a smile.

"And God still... loves us?!" questioned Rachel.

Leah, Rachel, and Esther sat quietly in deep thought before looking at one another with huge smiles.

"Maybe we can try cheesesteaks." said Esther.

"Or chicken parmesan." Leah suggested.

"Or cheeseburgers." Rachel proposed.

"Or taco with meat AND cheese!" they yelled together.

Soon students from nearby tables joined the conversation.

A little further down the table, Priya spoke up and shared, "In Hinduism, we have many gods and goddesses. One for wisdom, one for strength, one for money. Each one helps with something different."

Eden's eyes widened, "Wow, that's a lot to remember!" Everyone giggled. Then Eden smiled and said. "I believe in one God who does everything."

Priya tilted her head. "But why only one God in Christianity?"

Eden smiled. "Because the real God is enough. Plus He's the only true God. He made everything and everyone. And He loves us so much that He came to earth to save us. With Him, you have it all in one forever."

Another voiced chimed in softly. It was Jin. He inched close and said, "My family is Buddhist. We try to be really good, kinda like Rachel, Leah, and Esther, but we meditate so we can feel peace."

Eden nodded thoughtfully. "Jesus gives us peace too. When you know Him, He puts peace in your heart, even on the hardest days."

Jin looked curious. "So, Jesus helps even when things don't go the way we want?"

Eden nodded. "Yes! Jesus said we'll have troubles, but He also promised that He's with us always.' That means we're never alone, even when life feels scary or sad."

Jin smiled softly. "That sounds really comforting. Meditation helps me feel calm, but knowing Jesus is with me all the time sounds even better."

Nearby, Mateo raised his hand like in class.

"I'm Catholic," said Mateo. "In my family, we pray to Mary and the saints for help. We also light candles in church to feel close to God. That makes me feel peaceful."

Eden smiled warmly and said, "That's really nice that you want to feel close to God. I also like feeling close to Him. But, the Bible says Jesus is the only one who can truly bring us close to God."

"But don't you ask Mary for help? What about the saints or the Pope? Don't you need someone holy to help you get to God?" Mateo asked.

"No way!" Eden said, "Jesus doesn't need helpers to reach God. It's like if someone gave you a donut... you don't need a bunch of people to pass it around or take a bite before you can enjoy it. That donut is for you!" She leaned closer. "Same with Jesus. He's the only one who can bring us to God."

Maria, who was also Catholic, had been listening from another table. She stood shyly next to Mateo and asked Eden, "But if you don't have a Pope to tell you what God says, how do you know what's true or not?"

Eden turned to her and smiled. "That's a great question Maria! I learn what God says by reading the Bible myself. The Bible is God's own words, and it helps me understand Him and His love. Plus, I pray and ask the Holy Spirit to help me know what's true. Jesus promised the Holy Spirit would always guide us."

Maria smiled and nodded. "That makes sense. I guess it's kind of like when I read a recipe and follow the steps. Even if no one's there to watch me, I just trust the instructions to make the recipe right."
Maria looked thoughtful. "And praying for the Holy Spirit to help is like having a friend who explains the tricky parts. I like that!"

Caleb, who was a Jehovah's Witness, took a sip of his juice and said, "My family reads the Bible too, but we don't believe Jesus is God, We believe He's God's first creation."

Eden tilted her head. "Jesus couldn't have been created because the bible says He's always been here, and He created everything. And the bible also says that Jesus is God and Jesus is God's Son."

Caleb looked confused, "But how can He be God and God's Son?"

Eden said gently, "It's kind of like the sun in the sky. The sun and its light aren't two different things, they're both the sun. God the Father, Jesus the Son, and the Holy Spirit are all the one true God."

Noelle, another Jehovah's Witness quietly asked, "But what about Heaven? We are taught that only a small number people will get to live in Heaven with God."

Eden smiled. "Jesus said anyone who believes in Him will live with Him. That's not just a small number of people, it's everyone who trusts Him!

Noelle's eyes widened a little. "So... that means my friends and family could be there too?"

Eden nodded warmly. "Yes! God's invitation is for everyone. He wants the doors to Heaven to be wide open, not just for a small group. If we believe in Jesus and follow Him, we'll be with Him forever. "

Noelle smiled softly. "That would be amazing. I'd want all the people I love to be there with me."

Eden grinned. "Me too. That's why I love telling people about Jesus, so they can know the right way to Him."

Emma, who was Mormon, unwrapped her granola bar. "In my church, we believe Jesus is God's Son too. But we also believe in the Book of Mormon. We are taught that it's another Scripture from God, kind of like the Bible."

Eden nodded kindly. "I'm glad you believe Jesus is God's Son, but the Bible says God's Word is complete and can't be changed or added to. We don't need to add anything else because God's message through the Holy Bible is perfect and finished."

Emma nodded while chewing thoughtfully. "But don't you think there could be more teachings that help us understand God better?"

Eden shook her head gently. "I used to wonder that, but the Bible is from God and it should be used for teaching, correcting, and training us in righteousness. That means the Bible is enough to teach us everything we need to live the way God wants."

Priya's sister Ishani looked curious. "So, how do you know the Bible is true?"

Eden smiled brightly. "Because of Jesus! He fulfilled all the prophecies, and He died and came back to life to prove He's the Son of God."

Ishani smiled back. "That's really beautiful. I want to learn more about your Bible."

Suddenly Luna, who sat at the end of the table, held up a shiny crystal and said, "This crystal is supposed to bring me good luck and keep away bad vibes. My mom says it'll lead me to what is true."

Eden said, "That's cool, but peace, protection, and truth comes from Jesus, not stones. I get my peace and protection from Jesus. He's always with me, and nothing can block His power."

"Really?" Luna asked rubbing her crystal. "That sounds safer than hoping my crystal works."

Eden nodded. "It is. Jesus doesn't just hope to protect you or bring you peace, He promises to!"

Someone across the table twirled a tarot card. It was Imani. She and her sister were new to the school and always together.

Imani said, "Our mom uses tarot cards to tell the future. She says they can guide your life. Does Jesus guide you? Or do you use cards sometimes too?"

Eden shook her head. "Nope, I don't use cards. I just ask Jesus. He knows my whole life and He loves me more than anyone else. The Bible says He's the Good Shepherd who leads His sheep. That means when I follow Him, He guides me to what's best, even when I can't see the whole picture. It's not like guessing with cards or hoping for a lucky stone, it's knowing the One who actually made me and knows exactly what's ahead."

Imani's sister Amara sat thoughtfully and said, "But our mom says the spirits talk through her cards and spells. She says they give real answers. How do you know Jesus is better?"

Eden leaned forward a little. "Because Jesus isn't just a spirit, He's God. He made everything, including the spiritual world, and He has power over all of it. The Bible warns that some spirits can trick people, even if they sound nice at first. But Jesus can't lie, and He never tricks us. When I follow Him, I'm safe because He's stronger than anything else out there."

"Wait!" Tunde said as his eyes widened. "My father talks to spirits too! Sooo... if Jesus is stronger than everything, does that mean the spirits my father talks to can't hurt you? Even if they're really powerful?"

Eden nodded confidently. "Exactly. When you belong to Jesus, nothing in the spiritual world can hurt you without His permission. The Bible says He's like a fortress around us, totally unshakable. Evil spirits might try to scare people or tell lies, but they can't win against Jesus. It's kind of like being in the safest house in the world during a storm. You can hear the thunder, but you know you're completely safe inside because Jesus is guarding you."

Tunde's eyes grew wider. "Wow... that sounds really safe. I didn't know Jesus could do all of that."

Colton, who was atheist, shrugged with a skeptical smile and said, "I don't believe in anything really. Just science and stuff." He looked at Eden and asked, "How can you believe in something you can't see?"

Eden smiled. "It's kind of like Wi-Fi. You can't see it, but you know it's there because your tablet or phone works. Jesus is like that. You might not see Him with your eyes, but you can see what He does in people's lives."

Colton tilted his head. "So you're saying, you know He's there because of what happens when you trust Him?"

"Exactly," Eden said. "And just like Wi-Fi works better when you're connected, life works best when you're connected to Jesus."

"Wow, that actually makes perfect sense," Colton said.

Angelina tapped her fingers on the table. "But, how do you know it's true? I mean, lots of people believe different things. What if Jesus is just something people made up to feel better?"

Eden thought for a moment, then nodded. "That's a fair question. I believe it's true because Jesus really lived, really died, and really came back to life. There are hundreds of people that saw Him and wrote it down in the Bible. Plus so many people have researched Him, and proved He's real. You can even read about Him in history books."

Angelina tilted her head slightly. She wasn't sure she bought it, but something about Eden's confidence made her wonder if maybe, just maybe, there was more to the story than she thought.

"What about people who mess up?" asked Ravi.

"Everyone messes up," Eden said. "But Jesus doesn't give up on us, He helps us start again."

Ravi leaned in. "How?"

Eden grinned. "Like a video game! When you trust Jesus, it's like He gives you unlimited lives. He forgives your mistakes, helps you play better, and stays with you until you reach the best ending with Him."

"So, He doesn't get mad and leave?" asked Andy, whose eyebrows were wrinkled like he was afraid of the answer.

"No way," Eden said gently, shaking her head with a warm smile. "Jesus doesn't quit on people. He's always there, ready to forgive and help us grow. Even when we mess up, He doesn't storm off or cross His arms at us. He leans in closer to help us get back up."

Andy's eyes softened.

Eden continued, "It's like if you're learning to ride a bike and you fall, the person teaching you doesn't just walk away. They pick you up, steady you, and help you try again. That's what Jesus does, but for your whole life. Following Him isn't about being perfect, it's about knowing someone loves you no matter what."

Andy glanced at his sandwich but smiled just a little, like maybe he understood exactly what Eden meant.

At the edge of the table sat Ethan, the shy kid. He rarely ever spoke.

Ethan put his chin in his palms and leaned down on the table. "Sometimes I think we're just… here. Like we happened by accident. I don't know why." Ethan spoke quietly, but in his chest, a little ache stirred. The thought of the world being just a giant accident made him feel small, like a speck of dust floating in space with no direction.

Eden leaned forward, her tone soft but certain. "I used to wonder what I was here for too. But Jesus shows us that we were made on purpose, with a bunch of love. He gives our lives meaning and hope that never goes away."

For a second, Ethan didn't say anything. He wasn't sure he believed Eden, but something in those words made his chest feel just a little less heavy.

"Okay, okay, listen up!" yelled Clara, leaning forward with a huge grin on her face. "How about we all just pretend to be animals, like... I'll be a wise old owl, Mateo can be a tiger, and Zainab can be a dolphin. Then we can become one with nature and let our feelings guide us to be our own gods."

Everyone froze mid-bite, staring at her with wide, puzzled eyes.

Clara slowly stopped grinning. "Or... maybe that's not such a great plan?" she added, rubbing the back of her neck.

For a moment, there was silence. Then, Eden snorted, Esther let out a giggle, and soon the whole table erupted into laughter.

Clara laughed too, as her cheeks turned pink. "Fine, fine! No animal kingdom religions today. But, I'd still make a pretty awesome owl!"

Eden offered everyone a cookie from her lunchbox.

Jin took a bite and said, "Wow, that's good."

Eden grinned. "You know what's even better than cookies?"

"What?" Jin asked.

"Jesus!" Eden dipped her cookie in her milk and said, "The Bible says Jesus is the way, the truth, and the life. He came from Heaven, lived without doing anything wrong, died for us, and came back to life. And He did it because He loves us more than anyone ever could. All we have to do is believe in Him."

As the lunch bell rang, Rachel whispered, "Can you bring another bible verse tomorrow?"

Leah said, "Can I have one too?"

"Maybe one about peace?" Jin requested.

"Yeah, I want to hear more tomorrow." said Ishani with a smile.

"Let's all sit together again tomorrow," Yusuf said to everyone. Zainab, Mateo, Emma, Caleb and the others all cheered in agreement. Even Clara said, "Okay, I guess Jesus sounds like He might be kinda cool."

Eden smiled and nodded. "I'll bring more verses tomorrow. Maybe even extra cookies!" And in her heart, Eden whispered, "Thank You, Jesus, for lunch and for letting me share You with my new friends."

Also available from
Jude and John Publishing

The Good News of Jesus Christ presents the full gospel in clear, simple language, connecting the story of salvation from creation to the resurrection of Jesus so children gain clarity, confidence, and a strong foundation for understanding Scripture. Unlike many books that focus on Jesus as a friend or teacher, this story shows Him as He truly is: God in the flesh, the Savior of the world, and invites children to begin their walk with Christ rooted in truth and ready to share the good news. (Ages 5-9)

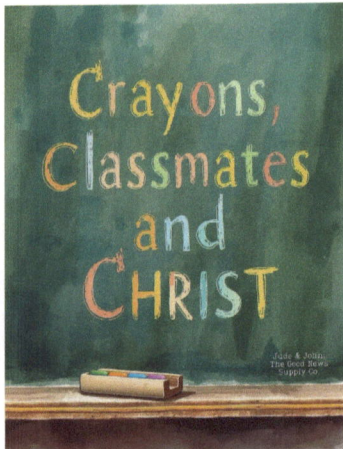

When Eden brings Jesus to show and tell, her classmates quickly discover that it is more than just another school presentation. With courage and clarity, Eden explains who Jesus is, why His death and resurrection matter, and what it means to believe in Him. Crayons, Classmates, and Christ shows children how to share the good news in a fun, simple, and age-appropriate way, helping them understand the gospel and speak about their faith with confidence. (Ages 5-9)

Jude and John, *The Good News Supply Co.*
www.JudeAndJohn.com

www.ingramcontent.com/pod-product-compliance
Lightning Source LLC
Chambersburg PA
CBHW042005100426
42736CB00038B/50